Bedrooms

30 instant bedroom transformations

Bedrooms

30 instant bedroom transformations

Stewart & Sally Walton

LORENZ BOOKS

First published in 1999 by Lorenz Books

© Anness Publishing Limited 1999

Lorenz Books is an imprint of
Anness Publishing Limited
Hermes House, 88–89 Blackfriars Road, London SE1 8HA

Distributed in Canada by Raincoast Books,
8680 Cambie Street, Vancouver, British Columbia V6P 6M9

ISBN 1 85967 924 2

Publisher: Joanna Lorenz
Senior editor: Lindsay Porter
Photographer: Graham Rae
Stylist: Catherine Tully
Designer: Simon Wilder
Jacket designer: Clare Baggaley

Printed in Hong Kong/China

1 3 5 7 9 10 8 6 4 2

CONTENTS

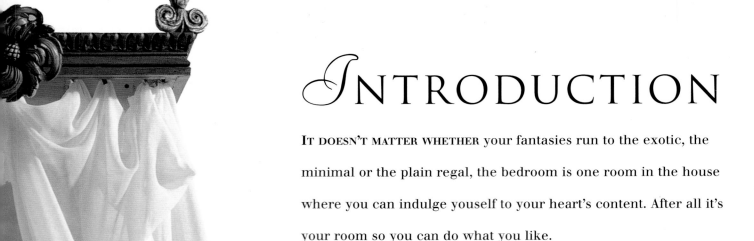

INTRODUCTION

IT DOESN'T MATTER WHETHER your fantasies run to the exotic, the minimal or the plain regal, the bedroom is one room in the house where you can indulge youself to your heart's content. After all it's your room so you can do what you like.

Whatever your tastes, our ideas rely more on imagination than money, more on practical inspirations than tool kit. And with our short cuts and great tips, decorating your bedroom won't put you to sleep. A good place to start is with the curtains. Tip number one: forget a curtain or fabric shop. Try instead a specialist sari shop. As soon as you enter you will be enveloped in colours you've only dreamt about. Imagine sunlight filtering through a window dressed with gossamer-light, deep-hued saris, the lightest breeze creating shimmers of movement among the golden threads.

Or perhaps you fancy a bedroom of cool serenity and creative order. This calls for Japanese inspiration: simple, uncluttered lines, plain fabrics and pale colours. A garden trellis covered with heavy tracing paper becomes a translucent screen, providing privacy with the softest light — the perfect solution for windows that open on to a blank wall.

A half-tester bed draped in cool white cotton adds romance and grandeur to any bedroom. It is simple and easy to create.

Once again, side-step traditional shops and head straight to a painter's supplier — decorator's dustsheets are incredibly inexpensive and a perfect covering for a futon mattress. Making the base is easier than you think. To cast a subtle light on your Oriental dreams, make a bedside lamp from corrugated card and bamboo skewers.

Sleep like a king or queen under a faux-carved half-tester and canopy. Shop-bought decorative wooden and plaster mouldings provide the fanciful trimmings and the gilded finishing touches, and the effect of filigree wall panelling can be created by using nothing more than simple radiator cover panels.

ℬED LINEN

Above: Canopies can be made with any lightweight material such as fine muslin or mosquito netting. Here, shells and seashore finds were attached at intervals to the fabric by drilling small holes into the items and stitching through.

ONE OF THE QUICKEST WAYS to revitalize a tired bedroom scheme is by changing the fabrics and colours that cover the bed – if you can stretch to new window treatments as well, you've got an instant make-over. Quick ideas such as these are ideal if you want a seasonal change: colourful wool blankets or heaps of velvet-covered cushions are cosy and inviting in the winter months, but might be overwhelmingly stifling when you want to throw open the windows on a summer morning. White muslin and crisp cotton is bright and breezy, evoking beach huts and summer holidays – light colours are always cool and calming.

Right: Bed linen complements this seaside-themed bedroom, with crisp cottons bordered in blue.

Splashes of colour can be incorporated into blanket edges or in simple patchwork, or picked out in embroidered motifs.

Take a good look at your bed linen – if you are not happy with it, it is very simple to change, and may be the starting point for a whole new decorating scheme.

Above: A metal day bed is made more inviting with heaps of pillows. Hand-embroidered motifs on the pillowcases add visual impact and their simple, linear style echoes the graceful lines of the ironwork.

Left: Nothing evokes country style like patchwork. Here, a traditional quilt pattern was teamed with sheets and pillowcases in contrasting checks. The careful choice of colours is what makes this mix-and-match approach so successful.

WALL TREATMENTS

THERE IS SO MUCH CHOICE on the market today in terms of paint effects and wallpapers that it is sometimes hard to know where to begin. Stencilling, stamping or stippling? Flat or broken colour? One way to approach the idea is to imagine what you would like the effect to be, and then investigate how it can best be achieved. Colour washes and glazes

Above: A paint roller was used to create the effect of hand-blocked wallpaper. Use a plumb line as a guide for straight lines. Stencil your chosen motif in the lighter stripes.

Right: Here, the walls complement the country look of the bed linen by using a motif based on a traditional patchwork design. The pattern is echoed on the surrounding furniture and accessories.

are great for less than perfect walls – the textured finish will appear to absorb any blemishes. Emphasize and make a virtue of an uneven surface by creating a plaster effect, or employ colour to make a large room cosy or a small room airy. These pages contain a few ideas to get you started.

Above: Colours at the cooler end of the spectrum are always a success in the bedroom. Soothing blues and calming greys used on the wall are carried through to the bed linen and furniture. Accents of colour (in this case red) are used sparingly, but prevent the whole scheme from becoming monotonous.

Left: The chalky rose of new plaster is warm and inviting – almost tactile. Here, it was used as the inspiration for the base colour on the wall. Heraldic motifs with a dropped-shadow effect were applied at regular intervals with a stamp cut from high-density foam rubber.

FINISHING TOUCHES

YOUR BEDROOM IS YOUR own private haven – so dare to indulge your decorating whims, simply because you can. Even a small bedroom can support judiciously chosen accessories or details – a tiny posy on a bedside table, a basket of old-fashioned pomanders, or a freshly laundered pile of bed linen all add to feelings of well-being and relaxation. Remember, this is perhaps the only room in the house where practicality need not be a prime consideration, and fantasy can be allowed to take over. Of course the bed is the centrepiece, but it can be

Above: A simple window treatment – creamy fabric hanging from looped tabs, threaded on to a length of wooden dowelling – is embellished with natural string tassels.

Right: Dried lavender has traditionally been used to keep linen smelling fresh. Here, circles of fabric has been cut out with pinking shears, filled with dried lavender and tied with co-ordinating lengths of ribbon. The resulting bundles are too pretty to be hidden away – keep a selection in a basket on a dressing table or window sill where the scent can freshen the air.

complemented and lifted dramatically by the right surroundings. These touches are so simple, yet special, that if you have a guest room it is worth incorporating them into the scheme. The room can be made so much more inviting at very little cost, and visitors will appreciate such welcoming gestures.

Above: Nothing lifts a room as instantly as fresh flowers – in the bedroom they seem particularly indulgent. Pots of hand cream and other lotions are decorated with circles of paper tied around the lids as an added touch.

Left: Piles of clean linen and hand towels are always welcome in a guest room, but make an equally pretty addition to the master bedroom. An enamel jug and bowl completes a country-themed bedroom – these can be found in junk shops and flea markets.

CANOPIED BED

A SIMPLE DRAPED CANOPY is a great way to define and decorate a sleeping area without completely enclosing it. Lightweight fabric is draped over a wooden plant support. The natural rustic character of the twigs combines very well with the unfussy appearance of the unbleached fabric. Muslin (cheesecloth) is inexpensive, so buy more than you need – any extra will make a pretty cascade at the end of the bed.

YOU WILL NEED

at least 12m (12 yd)
unbleached muslin
(cheesecloth)

iron-on hemming tape

iron

rustic plant support

rubber bands

twine

scissors

ceiling hook

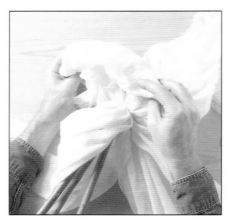

one *Turn up a hem at each end of the fabric and use iron-on hemming tape to make a neat hem. Find the middle of the fabric length and bunch and wrap the muslin around the narrow end of the plant support at this point.*

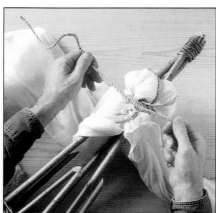

two *Pull the fabric into a pleasing shape, then secure it with rubber bands. Wind the twine to cover the rubber bands and decorate the fabric.*

three *Attach a ceiling hook centrally above the bed. Hang the plant support from it. Drape the muslin either side of the support and over the bed ends.*

HALF-TESTER

THIS POSITIVELY REGAL HALF-TESTER, draped with cool white cotton, will add majestic splendour to your bedroom. This sort of bed was popular around the second half of the nineteenth century, when fully-draped four-posters became less fashionable. The style imitates the ornate four-poster but is actually a box made to fit against the wall with a canopy that extends no more than a third of the length of the bed. This half-tester is made out of a batten and picture-frame moulding and adorned with plaster scrolls bought from a DIY store. The wall plaque is not strictly a part of the half-tester, but it adds the finishing touch. Use a fine white fabric, such as voile, muslin (cheesecloth) or cotton sheeting, for the drapes.

YOU WILL NEED

plaster-cast head wall hanging

backing paper

shellac

household paintbrushes

gold spray paint

black emulsion (latex) or poster paint

old, soft cloth

wire (steel) wool

2 scrolled plaster decorations

larger scrolled plaster decoration

155cm (62in) picture-frame moulding

wood stain (optional)

5 x 2.5cm (2 x 1in) batten, 115cm (46in) long

155cm (62in) door-frame moulding

saw

mitring block

glue gun and glue sticks

1cm (¾in) wooden dowelling, 10cm (4in) long

curtain rings with clips

heavy-duty staple gun or eyelet screws

at least 10m (11yd) fine white fabric

scissors

drill, with appropriate drill bit

wall plugs

screwdriver and long screws

one *Place the plaster-cast head on a piece of backing paper to protect your work surface. Apply a coat of shellac to seal the surface. Allow the first coat to dry (for about 20 minutes), then apply a second coat of shellac. Allow to dry.*

two *Spray the head with gold spray paint. Allow to dry. Paint over the gold with black emulsion (latex) or poster paint. Cover the gold completely.*

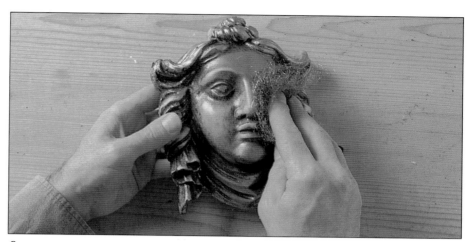

three *Before the paint dries, rub most of it off using a slightly damp cloth. The black will have dulled the brassiness of the gold beneath.*

four *Burnish the high spots, such as the cheek bones, nose and brows, using wire (steel) wool. Give the scrolled decorations and picture-frame moulding the same treatment, or stain them with your chosen colour of wood stain. Cut the batten into one 75cm (30in) and one 40cm (16in) length. Cut the door-frame and picture-frame mouldings into one 75cm (30in) and two 40cm (16in) lengths.*

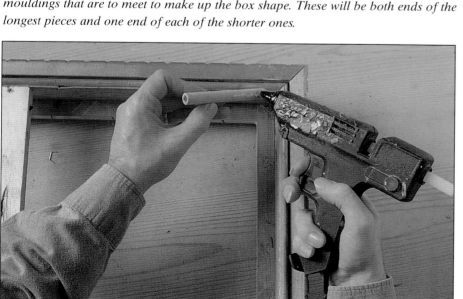

five *Using a mitring block, saw the corners on the door-frame and picture-frame mouldings that are to meet to make up the box shape. These will be both ends of the longest pieces and one end of each of the shorter ones.*

six *Glue the mitred door mouldings at the edges and fit the box shape together, placing the longest batten at the back. Surround the front three sides with the fancy moulding. Then glue the short batten in the centre of the piece as a reinforcement.*

seven *Cut the dowelling into two 5cm (2in) lengths and glue one piece into each top corner of the half-tester at the back of the moulding. They will act as supports for the scrolls.*

CONTINUED OVER ➤

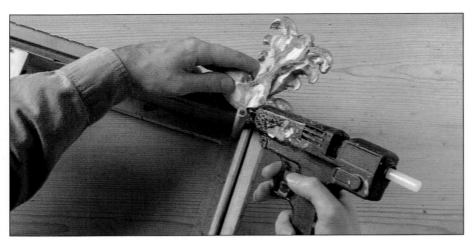

eight *Apply hot glue to each length of dowelling, and then stick the corner scroll decorations in place.*

nine *Fix the curtain rings with clips at equal distances around the inside of the mouldings, using a heavy-duty staple gun or eyelet screws.*

ten *Cut the fabric in half along its length. Before putting up the half-tester, clip one length of fabric around one side to see how much fabric falls between each pair of clips. It will be easier to hang the drapes once the half-tester is in place if you have worked out the spacing in advance. Remove the fabric. Fix the half-tester to the wall near the ceiling, using appropriate fixings, and fix the plaster head to the wall. Clip the drapes in place and drape the fabric around the bed.*

ROMANTIC NETTING

EVEN IF YOU HAVE NO practical need for mosquito netting, the light and airy beauty of this project makes it ideal for the bedrooms of urban romantics who dream of being in the Punjab or on the Serengeti plains. Netting like this can be bought from camping shops and comes complete with a spoked wooden coronet that opens like a fan to support it. Here, the spokes have then been decorated with dangling glass ornaments to make the netting look more exotic than utilitarian. Plain white netting is very appealing, but it can also be dyed in any colour.

YOU WILL NEED

mosquito netting, with coronet and fixings

dangling glass ornaments and earrings

fine wire

long-nosed pliers

ceiling hook

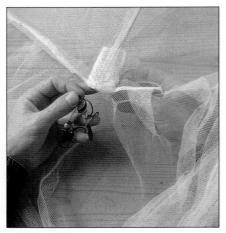

one *Fan out the spokes of the wooden coronet and fit them into the channels of the netting.*

two *Thread assorted glass ornaments, beads and earrings on to lengths of fine wire to make decorative pendants.*

three *Thread the wire ends through the netting at the bottom of the spokes. Use long-nosed pliers to twist the ends together to secure them.*

four *Attach the ring and rope provided to the centre of the coronet. Hang the net from a ceiling hook above the bed.*

FOUR-POSTER SARI

THE DRAPES FOR THIS four-poster bed have been made from lengths of beautifully coloured traditional sari fabric and ribbons. Whether wrapped, folded or tucked, they do not appear at all bulky. Most saris have border designs and end pieces, with quite plain central areas. The saris used here are made from organza (organdie), and the yellow and orange panels have been hung alternately around three sides of the bed.

YOU WILL NEED

8 sari lengths
dressmaker's pins
needle
matching sewing threads
15m (16½yd) ribbon or braid
scissors
tape measure
self-adhesive velcro dots (optional)
1 x 1m (1yd) silk fabric
square cushion tassels (optional)

one *Pin and sew a length of ribbon or braid along the top of each sari to reinforce the fabric. Cut six 30cm (12in) lengths of ribbon or braid per sari for loops. Pin the ribbon lengths along the top of each sari, about 30cm (12in) apart. Turn under one end of each ribbon and slip-stitch to the sari, leaving the other end loose.*

two *Hang the saris from the four-poster. Loop the ribbons around the rail. Sew the loose ends with a few small slip-stitches, or use self-adhesive velcro dots.*

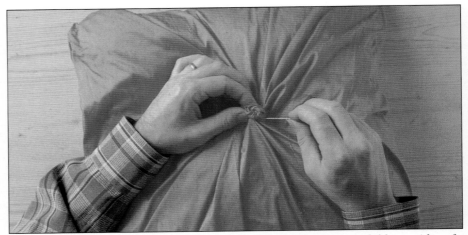

three *Place the cushion pad in the centre of the fabric. Loosely fold two sides of the fabric over it, then fold the other two sides over them. Slip-stitch the back seam, but do not pull the fabric tightly around the cushion pad. Turn the cushion over. Pull up the fabric in the centre and twist into a decorative knot. Hold the knot in place with a few stitches. Decorate with tassels in a similar shade if desired.*

INDIAN TEMPLE BEDHEAD

INDIAN TEMPLE WALL PAINTINGS are the inspiration for this arch-shaped bedhead. The bedroom feels as if it has been magically transported thousands of miles, but the real magic here comes in a simple pot of paint. Before painting the bedhead, set the mood with a deep rust-coloured wash on the walls. If you can, use a water-based distemper for an authentic powdery bloom. If you are using emulsion (latex), thin it with water.

YOU WILL NEED

large roll of brown parcel wrap

felt-tipped pen

masking tape (optional)

scissors

spray adhesive

chalk

water-based paint: dark blue, bright blue and red

plate

kitchen sponge

cream emulsion (latex)

medium and fine paintbrushes

fine-grade sandpaper

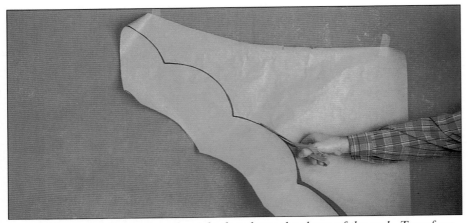

one *Refer to the diagram on the right that shows the shape of the arch. Transfer a half-arch on to brown parcel wrap, enlarging it as required using a grid system. Alternatively, tape a sheet of brown parcel wrap on the wall and draw the half-arch directly on to it, following the pattern shape.*

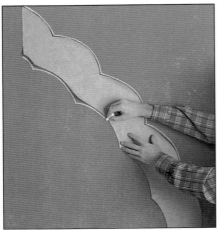

two *Cut out the half-arch shape, using a pair of scissors. Position the paper pattern on the wall with spray adhesive and draw around the edges with chalk.*

three *Flip the pattern and draw around it to produce the second half of the arch. Spread some dark blue paint on to a plate and use a damp sponge to dab it on to the central panel. Don't cover the background completely, but leave some of the wall colour showing through. When the paint is dry, apply the bright blue paint over the dark blue in the same way.*

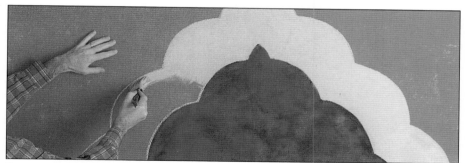

four *When the paint is dry, paint the arch in sandy cream emulsion, using a medium-sized paintbrush. When the emulsion paint is dry, rub it back in places with fine-grade sandpaper to give a faded effect. Outline the inside and outside of the arch with the red paint, using a fine paintbrush. Support your painting hand with your free hand and use the width of the brush to make a single line. Outline the inner red stripe with a thinner dark blue line.*

five *Leave to dry, then use fine-grade sandpaper to soften any hard edges and give the arch the naturally faded appearance of an old temple wall.*

BEACH MAT BED

A SIMPLE FOUR-POSTER FRAME can be built to fit around an existing base and mattress. This requires only basic carpentry skills as the timber can be cut to size when you buy it, and just needs drilling and screwing together. The wood used here is basic construction timber that has been left in its natural state, but you could colour it with woodstain or paint it to co-ordinate with the decor of the bedroom.

Grass beach mats are perfect for hanging around the four-poster, especially if your room is decorated with natural fabrics and earth colours. The loosely stitched grass strips allow a soothing, soft golden light to filter through and the air to circulate.

YOU WILL NEED

grass beach mats

packet of brass paper fasteners

rough twine

scissors

selection of shells, pebbles and driftwood

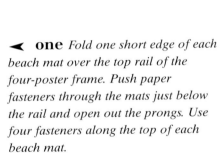

◄ **one** *Fold one short edge of each beach mat over the top rail of the four-poster frame. Push paper fasteners through the mats just below the rail and open out the prongs. Use four fasteners along the top of each beach mat.*

two *The mats are edged with coloured tape that makes fine stripes around the bed. Arrange the mats to make the most of this striping.* ►

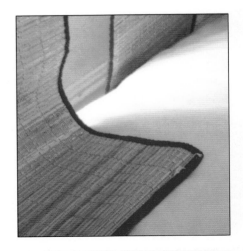

three *Decide how many blinds you want to tie up – maybe all, or just a select few. You will need about 1m (1yd) of rough twine for each mat to be rolled up. Cut the lengths required and tie some shells, pebbles and bits of driftwood randomly along the length and at each end of the twine.*

four *Dangle over the top rail and use them to tie back the rolled-up blinds.*

JAPANESE FUTON

THIS STYLISH AND UNCLUTTERED bedroom exudes a typically Japanese sense of simplicity, order and tranquillity. Wooden pallets were used to make the bed base. These come in different sizes, but they can be sawn down and stacked to get the right size. The beautiful cream cotton bedcover is, unbelievably, a decorator's dust sheet, embellished with knotted cords. Dust sheets like this are incredibly cheap, so you can have the minimalist look for a minimal outlay. Just add a pillow and a cushion – and sleep well!

YOU WILL NEED

wooden pallets

medium- and fine-grade sandpaper

light-coloured woodstain

household paintbrush

2m (2yd) black cotton cord

scissors

needle

matching sewing thread

decorator's dust sheet

2 black tassels

square cream-coloured cushion

one *Rub down the wooden pallets, using first medium-grade, then fine-grade sandpaper. Apply a coat of light-coloured woodstain to seal and colour the wood. Lay the pallets on the floor to make a bed base.*

two *Cut six 30cm (12in) lengths of black cotton cord. Make each length into a loop tied with a reef knot.*

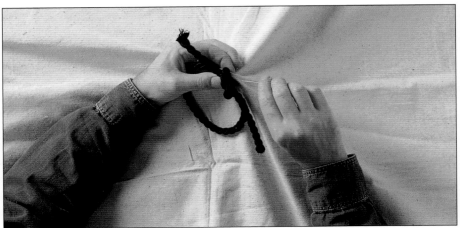

three *Slip-stitch the knotted cords on to the dust sheet to make three rows of two cords down the centre of the bed. Spread the dust sheet on the bed and fold it neatly over the pillows. Sew two black tassels on to the cushion and place it on the pillows. Tuck the dust sheet under the mattress all the way around the bed.*

CALICO TENT

GET THAT HOLIDAY FEELING every morning when you look out on the day from your tent. This could make a novelty bedhead for a child's bedroom or a stylish feature in a adult's bedroom. The tent is made using a combination of fittings intended for different purposes. The chrome rods are shower rails, finished off in copper with plumber's pipe caps. The thin copper tube is also from the plumbing department – it has an attractive finish and can be bent easily with long-nosed pliers. The stability of the tent is assured by the use of shower rail sockets on the wall and a line of cup hooks on the ceiling. The fabric used here is unbleached calico.

YOU WILL NEED

8 x 1m (8¾ x 1yd) unbleached calico

tape measure

pencil and ruler

scissors

6m (6½yd) iron-on hemming tape

iron

hacksaw

150cm (60in) length of chrome shower rail

centre punch

hammer

drill, with bit (the size of the copper tube)

1m (1yd) narrow copper tube

long-nosed pliers

3 chrome shower rail sockets

spirit (carpenter's) level

screwdriver

6 chrome cup hooks and wall plugs

4m (4½yd) white cord

3 copper pipe caps (to fit shower rail)

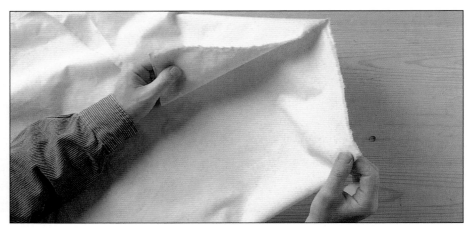

one *Decide on the height of the top of the tent. Measure off the fabric and tear it to size. Fold the fabric in four to find the centre and mark this point. Measure 36cm (14in) down each short edge and mark the points.*

two *Draw a connecting line between the centre point and each of the side points to give the shape for the top.*

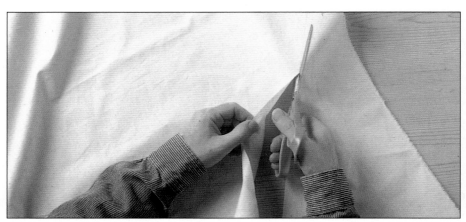

three *Cut along the drawn lines, then cut a 3cm (1¼in) notch at each of the points of the tent shape. Fold the fabric over to make a 3cm (1¼in) seam around the top and sides of the fabric.*

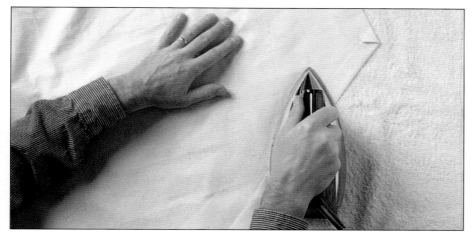

four *Use iron-on hemming tape to hold down the seams neatly. The two pieces should now meet at a right angle to make the tent shape. The sides and top of the tent will fold back to give a double thickness of fabric. Make three holes for the rails at the corner points and reinforce the fabric with an extra square of calico ironed on with hemming tape.*

five *Use a hacksaw to cut the length of chrome shower rail into three 50cm (20in) pieces.*

six *Use a centre punch to dent the shower rail where the holes will be drilled, so that the drill does not slip. You will need to drill a hole 5cm (2in) from one end of two of the poles and two holes in the other pole, the first 5cm (2in) from one end and the second 1cm (½in) in from it.*

seven *Drill the holes using a drill bit the same size as the copper tube. Use a hacksaw to cut two lengths of copper tube. Use the long-nosed pliers to bend one end of each copper tube into a hook shape. Use the chrome rail to estimate the curve of the hooks. Each hook should fit snugly around the chrome rail with its end fitting into the drilled hole.*

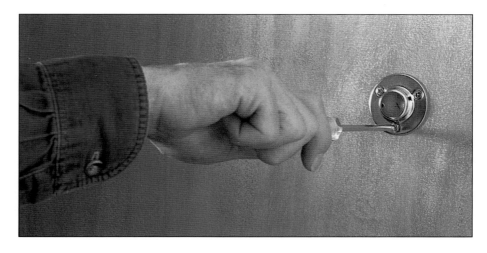

eight *Position the shower rail sockets on the wall so that the rails slot into them. Use a spirit (carpenter's) level to check that the outer two are level.*

CONTINUED OVER ➤

Above: The hooked copper tubes fit over and into the chrome rail. The cord is looped around the rail and crossed over to suspend the tent front from the cup hooks. The side rail is finished off with the copper cap and suspended from a crossed cord attached to the cup hooks.

nine *Refer to the diagram below. Push the chrome rails through the holes in the back of the tent, then fit the copper tubes in place to hold the front section rigid. Fit the straight end of each copper tube into the hole in each side rail. Fit the hooked ends over the middle rail and into the two drilled holes. Fix a row of cup hooks to the ceiling directly above the front edge of the tent. Loop white cord around the cup hooks and the chrome rails for added stability. Finally, cap the chrome pipes with the copper caps.*

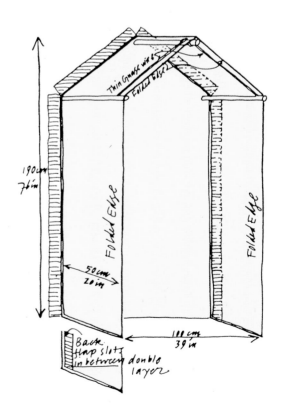

RENAISSANCE HEADBOARD

DRAMATIC EFFECTS HAVE BEEN used in this bedroom to create a very distinctive atmosphere, with the large painting dominating the room. It's a good idea to visit a museum shop for the best range and quality of art posters – you are certain to find something for all tastes. You can apply a crackle glaze or antiquing varnish to the poster if you wish to add an authentically aged Renaissance look.

one *Mix up the wallpaper paste. Mark the position of the poster on the backing board and apply paste to that section. Smooth the poster on to the board and leave to dry. Any air bubbles should disappear as the glue dries.*

two *Measure and mark the lengths of moulding for the frame. It goes along the top of the poster and down both sides to mattress height. Saw the corners on a mitring block. Paint a green undercoat. Leave to dry.*

three *Protect your work surface, then spray a coat of gold spray paint over the green. Leave to dry. Rub the frame with fine-grade sandpaper, so that the gold is lifted on the highest ridges to reveal the green beneath. Do not overdo the sanding. Use a glue gun to stick the picture frame around the edges of the poster.*

four *Paint the whole surface of the poster with crackle-glaze varnish, following the manufacturer's instructions. Leave the varnish to crackle. Use a cloth to rub artist's oil colour into the surface. Red is used here but any strong or dark colour will also work well. Rub the oil paint right into the cracks and cover the whole surface.*

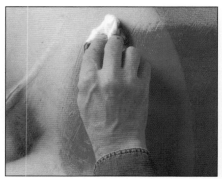

five *Rub the oil paint off the surface with a soft cloth. The colour will stay in the cracks. Apply several coats of clear varnish to the poster. When dry, attach the headboard to the bed frame, using the drill and fixtures.*

GINGHAM HEADBOARD

THIS HEADBOARD CONVERSION creates a fresh new style with added comfort. Gingham always looks crisp and bright, so you will wake up bright-eyed and ready to face the day. It is available in both small and large checked patterns and in a wide variety of both bright and pastel colours. The gingham is backed with wadding (batting). Alternatively, you could use other fabrics to create a different sort of mood – a small floral print for a feminine, country cottage decor or a vibrant primary colour for a teenager's room, for example. The headboard should be rectangular in shape and can be solid or of a slatted or spindled type. Measure the width and height of the headboard, then double the height measurement so that the gingham folds in half over the top.

YOU WILL NEED

iron-on quilter's wadding (batting)

scissors

iron

gingham, width of the headboard x twice the height, plus seam allowance on all edges

iron-on hemming tape or needle and matching sewing thread

2m (2yd) red ribbon

dressmaker's pins

tape measure

one *Cut the wadding (batting) to the size of the headboard. Press one end of the gingham on to the wadding. The other end of the gingham will fold over the headboard back. Leave a large seam allowance all around the edge.*

two *Fold the seams over and tuck the corners in neatly. Use iron-on hemming tape or a needle and thread to secure the edges. As the hems will be on the inside of the cover, they will not be visible.*

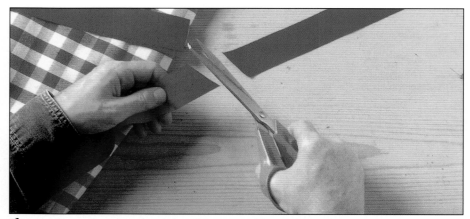

three *To make the ties, cut the ribbon into 16 equal lengths.*

four *Pin, then sew four ribbons, equally spaced, along the inside edges of each side of the cover. Fold the cover over the headboard and tie the ribbons in bows to finish.*

CHINTZ HEADBOARD

GIVE YOUR PADDED HEADBOARD a new lease of life using old chintz curtains. The fabric improves with age as the colours fade and mellow delightfully, and it looks wonderful teamed with crisp white cotton, handmade quilts or plaid woollen blankets in a traditional bedroom. Use the very best section of pattern for the bedhead and tuck remaining lengths under the mattress to form a valance. If you prefer a more permanent valance, you could sew pleated lengths of the same chintz fabric around the edges of a fitted sheet.

YOU WILL NEED

pair of floral chintz curtains
scissors
tape measure
headboard
pencil
staple gun and staples

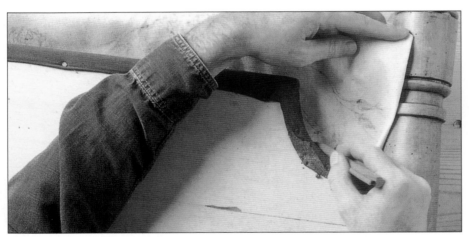

one *Trim the curtains to get rid of any thick seams, curtain tape and bulky hems. Cut a strip of curtain long enough to fold over the front and on to the back of the headboard at the sides, top and bottom. Smooth it over the front of the headboard then move to the back. Draw any curved corners on to the back of the fabric.*

two *Cut notches in the fabric right up to the drawn line, so that the fabric will fit the curve without puckering. Staple each cut strip on to the headboard.*

three *Pull down the top flap tautly and staple it on to the headboard.*

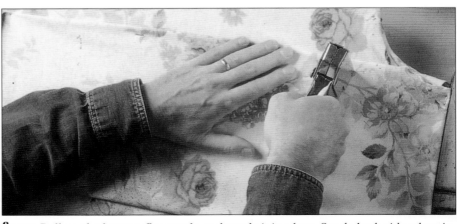

four *Pull up the bottom flap tautly and staple it in place. Staple both side edges in the same way. Cut a panel of fabric to cover all the stapled edges on the back. Turn in the edges and staple the panel flat on to the backing board.*

DREAM TRELLIS

DRESS UP A PLAIN WALL behind a simple bed with an unusual trellis headboard made from woven twigs and branches. The trellis is very lightweight and is easily fixed in place. Continue the theme with twig accessories, ranging from chairs to cache-pots, and complement the decor with crisply starched white sheets and pretty cushion covers.

Country garden centres are always worth a visit, because trellis-work like this is handmade and producers often use local garden centres as outlets. Alternatively, you might like to try to make your own.

YOU WILL NEED

garden raffia

scissors

handmade twig trellis

masonry nails or
cavity wall fixtures

hammer

one *Divide the raffia into two bunches of approximately 12 strands each. Knot one end of each bunch.*

two *Plait (braid) the strands to make two braids about 10cm (4in) long.*

three *Tie the plaits on to the trellis 25cm (10in) from each end. Attach the plaits to the wall above the bed, suspending the trellis behind the bed.*

ENTWINED HEADBOARD

QUITE APART FROM BEING one of the most stylish looks around, rope wrapping is a real pleasure to do. All you need is a frame, which can be a junk-shop find or a DIY structure made from construction timber. The wood is completely hidden by the coils of rope, so there is no need to prepare the surface in any way. Rope comes in many different twists and thicknesses, some more decorative than others. Some ropes are made from natural fibres and others, like the one used here, are synthetic. An advantage of synthetic rope is that the ends can be sealed by holding them over a flame to melt the fibres together.

YOU WILL NEED

rope

wooden-framed headboard

tape measure

pen

scissors or craft knife

cutting mat or thick cardboard

lighter or matches (optional)

glue gun and glue sticks

one *To calculate the length of rope needed to wrap each wooden post, first divide the height of the post by the thickness of the rope. Multiply this figure by the circumference of the post. Mark the rope at this point.*

two *Cut the lengths of rope required to wrap all the posts. If you are using synthetic rope, seal the ends by holding them briefly over a flame. Use the glue gun to stick the end of the rope to the back of the first post to be wrapped.*

three *Wrap the rope tightly around the post, keeping the coils as close together as possible. To maintain the tension, apply a few dabs of hot glue.*

four *Cut short lengths of rope to cover gaps and another to cover loose ends and blobs of glue at the intersection. Glue the ends at the back.*

five *Make sure that all the intersections are finished in the same way so that the symmetry is maintained.*

SHEER MAGIC

TRIM A PLAIN LINEN or hessian bed cover and pillowcase with the sheerest of voile fabrics to give a look that is simple, tailored and elegant. Large bone buttons and the rougher textures of hessian and linen are the perfect foil to the fineness of the fabric. Cut the voile slightly longer than the drop on the bed so it falls on to the floor all around. The amount of voile given here is for a double bed, but the idea can be adapted to suit any bed size.

YOU WILL NEED

tape measure

about 7m (7½yd) cotton voile

scissors

dressmaker's pins

needle

tacking (basting) thread

sewing machine

matching sewing thread

hessian (burlap) or fine linen bed cover

16 large bone buttons

fine embroidery scissors

tapestry needle

fine string

pillow, and hessian to cover

hessian or fine linen

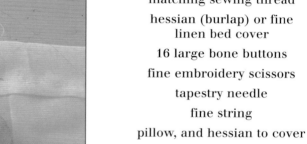

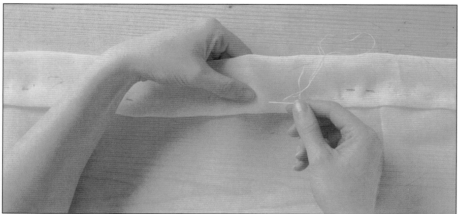

one *For the top of the cover, you will need a piece of voile the length of the bed plus the drop on one end. The piece should be 15cm (6in) narrower than the width of the bed so the buttons will not be too near the edge. Allow 10cm (4in) all round for double hems. For the sides, you will need two pieces the length of the bed. Measure the drop from the buttons to the floor, allowing 10cm (4 in) for hems as before. Pin, tack and sew all the hems.*

two *Mark the position of the buttons and buttonholes. They must correspond exactly. Sew the buttonholes then cut the centres carefully. Use a tapestry needle and fine string to sew the buttons in position on the hessian (burlap) bed cover, and button the voile cover on top.*

three *For the pillowcase, cut a piece of hessian (burlap) the depth of the pillow and twice the length, plus seam allowances on the long sides. With right sides together, pin, tack and sew the top and bottom edges. Turn right-side out and press.*

four *To make a fringed edge, find a thread running across the pillow, just in from the cut edge. Pull gently to fray the edge. Use the same method to make an over-cover for the pillow from voile. Hem all the edges.*

five *Mark the position of the button-holes in each corner. Machine-stitch the button-holes and cut the centres. Sew buttons on to the corners of the hessian pillow cover, and button the voile cover over the top.*

Victorian Lace

NOTHING LOOKS MORE ROMANTIC and feminine than a brass bed covered with snowy white, lace-trimmed bed linen. Make layers of scallops and frills on sheets, bolsters, pillows and bedcovers. Start by buying a good cotton duvet cover with a scalloped edge. Trawl second-hand shops and flea markets for lace-edged tablecloths, dressing table runners, tray cloths and curtain panels. Look out for old white cotton sheets with embroidered edges to add interest.

YOU WILL NEED

plain white bed linen

selection of lacy tablecloths, tray cloths, mats, chair backs or dressing table runners

dressmaker's pins

iron

iron-on hemming tape or needle and white thread

bolsters

rubber bands

white ribbon or raffia

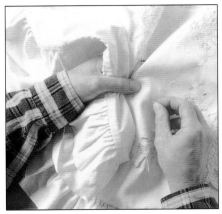

one *Select suitably sized lace additions to make central panels or corner details on the pillow-cases and duvet cover. Pin them in position.*

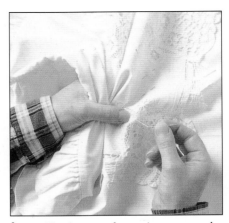

two *Use iron-on hemming tape and an iron to bond the two layers together, or slip-stitch them in place.*

three *Roll the bolster up in a lace-edged tablecloth and bunch up the ends, securing them with rubber bands. Tie ribbon or raffia over the gathered ends and drape the lace edging.*

LOVELY LINENS

PRETTY UP PERFECTLY PLAIN LINENS with splashes of vibrant colour. To add definition, run strips of rick-rack edging around; for frilliness, buy broderie anglaise and sew this on to the pillowcase. You could weave tapestry yarn through the broderie in place of ribbon, to add colour. Alternatively, look for linens which have a fine-holed edging and thread through this with fine tapestry yarn. To complement the edges, add tiny decorative crosses to buttons sewn on to the pillowcase. A more time-consuming, but extremely effective decoration is made by scalloping the edge of a sheet and decorating with tapestry yarn.

YOU WILL NEED

paper
pencil
cardboard
scissors
single or double white sheet
sewing machine
white sewing thread
small, sharp-pointed scissors
red tapestry yarn
tapestry needle
plain pillowcase
3m (3yd) broderie anglaise
dressmaker's pins
buttoned pillowcase, with
fine-holed decorative edge
glue gun and glue sticks
decorative red buttons

one *Cut out a cardboard template for the sheet edging. Draw around it then machine satin-stitch over the line. Cut along outside the sewn line.*

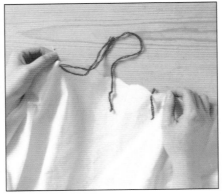

two *Cut lengths of coloured tapestry yarn and knot the ends. Sew the lengths of yarn through the sheet leaving the long ends as decoration.*

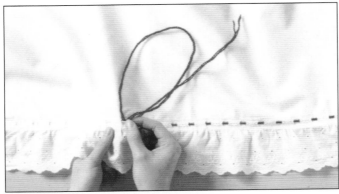

three *Edge the plain pillowcase with broderie anglaise. Then use a tapestry needle to thread coloured yarn through the holes in the lace. You can also use this technique to decorate pillowcases with fine-holed decorative edging.*

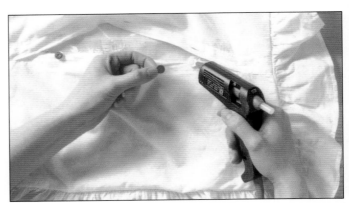

four *You can liven up plain buttons on a pillowcase by using a glue gun to apply decorative coloured buttons on top. Decorate round cloth buttons by making neat cross-stitches over them with tapestry yarn.*

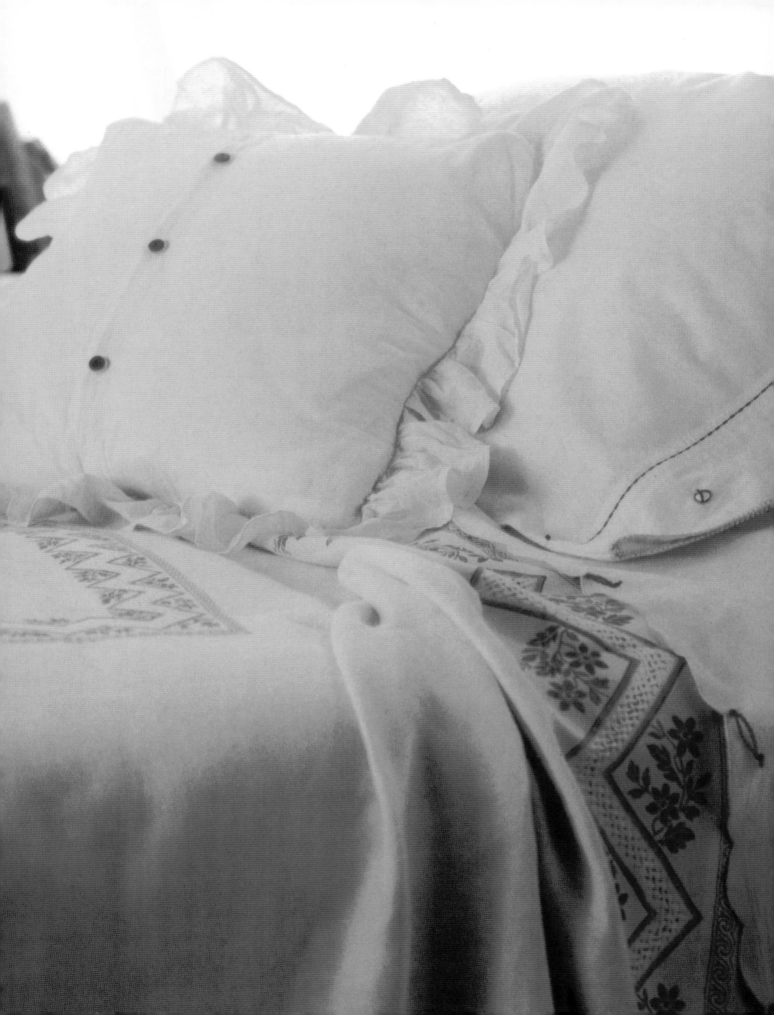

*L*OVE PILLOWS

MAKE SURE THE RIGHT message gets across by stencilling the word 'love' on your pillows in both English and French, the archetypal language of romance! The typeface used is the graphic designer's favourite, Gill (bold), chosen for its stylish simplicity and clarity. There is no doubt what is meant here. The word has been enlarged on a photocopier to 18cm (7in) long. You can adapt this idea for other messages that are completely personal and private, but if you have children, discretion may be a good idea. Choose colours that match your bedroom's overall scheme or that are your favourites. Fabric paints are available in a wide range of colours. Always wash and iron the fabric before stencilling to rid it of any glazes that could block the colour absorption.

YOU WILL NEED
photocopied enlargement
of letters
spray adhesive
2 pieces of stencil cardboard
scalpel or craft knife
cutting mat or thick cardboard
sheet of thin cardboard
white cotton pillowcases
fabric paint
old plate
stencil brush
iron

one *Enlarge the templates to the required size. Spray the backs of the photocopies with spray adhesive and stick them on to the stencil card.*

two *Cut out the letters on a cutting mat. The O, A and R need ties to retain the internal letter features, so draw them in "bridges" before you cut out.*

three *Place a sheet of thin cardboard inside the pillow case, so that the colour does not bleed through to the other side.*

four *Apply paint sparingly to letters. You can always build up colour later, but too much paint can cause problems. When dry, seal with a hot iron.*

AEOL
MRUV

AMERICAN DREAM

LIE IN STATE EVERY NIGHT, draped in a Stars and Stripes-patterned quilt or any brightly coloured flag design that takes your fancy. This is a great bed-covering idea and different rooms can have different flags to complement different colour schemes. The timber-clad walls and peg-rail above the bed give the room a ranch-house feel that looks great alongside brilliant red, white and blue.

YOU WILL NEED

flag-patterned fabric
pillow
safety pins
wooden buttons
needle and matching thread
quilt

one *Fold a piece of flag-patterned fabric around the pillow and use safety pins to close the long seam.*

two *Sew three wooden buttons along one pillow edge to hold the seam closed. Leave the other edge open so the pillow can be removed.*

three *Select an assortment of wooden buttons to attach around the edge and across the centre of a second piece of fabric.*

four *Lay the fabric over the quilt. Sew on the buttons, stitching through both the fabric and the quilt, so that the layers are held together.*

HAMMOCK QUILT

RECLINING IN A HAMMOCK MAY BE THE ULTIMATE relaxation, but it is only really possible to lie back and enjoy the sway if you feel completely secure. So make quite sure that your wall fittings are sturdy and properly installed and that the wall itself is strong enough to take the strain. Use strong metal garage hooks with long screws and heavy-duty wallplugs. Once the safety angle has been covered, you can then turn your attention to comfort and make this stylish and simple no-sew quilt to dress up your hammock and keep you cosy.

YOU WILL NEED

iron

2.5m (2¾yd) iron-on wadding (batting)

5m (5½yd) blue fabric

2.5m (2¾yd) black cotton fabric

scissors

tape measure

iron-on hemming tape

5m (5½yd) black iron-on mending tape

dressmaker's pins

one *Iron the wadding (batting) to one half of the wrong side of the blue fabric. Then fold the other half over so that the wadding is sandwiched by the blue fabric. This will give the quilt some thickness. Next, cut the black fabric into four 14cm (5½in) wide strips to fit the quilt edges. Press a 1cm (½in) hem along the long edges. Iron each strip in half to make a long doubled strip 6cm (2¼in) wide. This will be used to border the blue cloth. Place a length of iron-on hemming tape along each edge of the blue fabric and enclose each edge with a doubled black border strip. Iron to bond the fabrics. Fold down the corners of the black edging to achieve a mitred effect. Turn the fabric over and repeat on the other side.*

two *Cut 24 x 20cm (8in) strips of iron-on mending tape and use the tape measure to position them on the quilt in four rows of three crosses.*

three *Pin the crosses in place if required, then iron them in position.*

BLACK AND WHITE PRINTS

IMAGINE BEING ABLE to decorate soft furnishings with any image or picture of your choice. There is now a special transparent gel available which enables you to transfer black and white or colour images on to fabric. The image can then be sealed to make it resistant to wear and tear. By enlarging or reducing the images on a photocopier, you can obtain a selection of prints that will fit perfectly on to any item that you would like to decorate, such as cushions, pillows or even a quilt. You can use the same process to monogram your bed linen in royal style. However, because the image will be reversed once it is transferred, you will have to photocopy any lettering on to acetate first.

YOU WILL NEED

photocopies of chosen images

scissors

plain-coloured cotton cushion cover

iron

plastic carrier bag

image-transfer gel

small household paintbrush

soft cloth

sheet of acetate (optional)

one *Choose your images and make the required number of copies. Here, several copies of the same image are used to form a frame around the portrait.*

two *Cut away all the excess paper, leaving only the images that you want to transfer.*

three *To design the cushion cover, arrange the images on a flat surface. Experiment with spacing until you are happy with the design.*

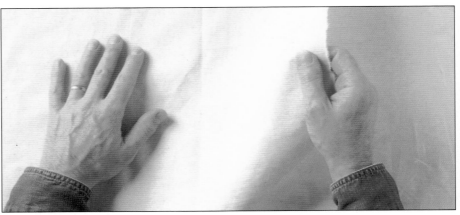

four *Pre-wash and iron the cushion cover. This is important because glazes used to stiffen fabrics may adversely affect the transfer process. Place the cover on a plastic carrier bag to protect your work surface.*

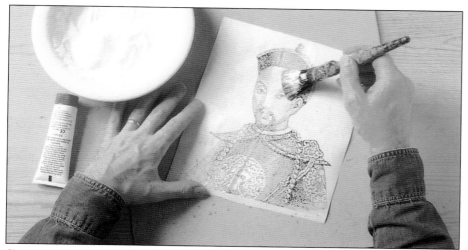

five *Paint a thick layer of transfer gel on to the first photocopy, making sure that you have covered it completely.*

six *Place the image face-down in position on the cushion cover and gently rub all over the back with a soft cloth. Leave the image in position.*

seven *Repeat steps 5 and 6 with all the images, ensuring that they are positioned accurately before you make contact with the fabric. Leave to transfer overnight.*

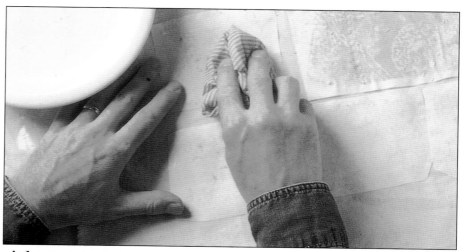

eight *Soak the cloth with clean water and then use the wet cloth to saturate the photocopy paper.*

nine *Keep the cloth wet and begin to rub away the paper, working from the centre outwards. The images will have transferred on to the fabric. When all the paper has been removed, leave the fabric to dry.*

ten *Apply a final fixing coat of the transfer gel to the prints and leave to dry completely.*

CONTINUED OVER ➤

eleven *You can use the same process to monogram your bed linen. Photocopy the initials on to a sheet of acetate. Then turn the acetate over and photocopy from the acetate on to paper to reverse. Cut out the print.*

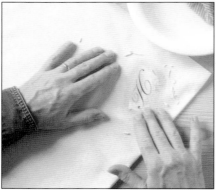

twelve *Transfer the initials as described in steps 5 to 10. The transfer process will reverse the initials once more, so that they are now the right way round.*

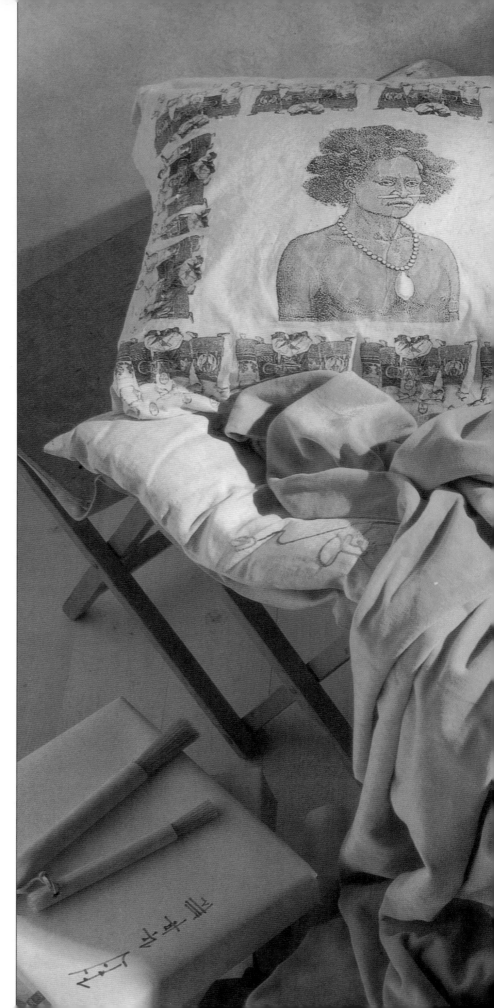

COPYCATS

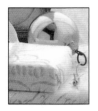

CREATE A TRULY BEAUTIFUL setting by mixing fine, snowy-white linens, soft, filmy voile and crunchy tissue paper with gold lettering and initials. It looks extremely impressive and, although quite time-consuming, is easy to execute. Use any kind of calligraphy that appeals to you. (Here, the frontispiece from some sheet music was used.) Photocopy and enlarge your choice and trace it on to the voile, linen and tissue paper.

YOU WILL NEED

typeface or script samples
(e.g. from a calligraphy
book)

voile for curtain

masking tape

gold fabric paint

fine paintbrushes

iron

tissue paper

gold acrylic paint

organza (organdie) ribbon

linen hand towel

carbon paper or soft pencil
(optional)

hard pencil (optional)

one *Select different types of script samples. You may not find everything you need from one source, so look out for individual details. Photocopy the script samples, enlarging them to size. Experiment by moving the pieces of script around to create pleasing combinations and arrangements. Position the photocopies on the voile for the curtain, devising a pattern along its length.*

two *Tape your photocopy to a table or work surface, ensuring it is flat. Tape the fabric on top, so you can see the script through it. Using gold fabric paint and a fine paintbrush, trace the lettering on to the voile. Press the fabric, following the manufacturer's instructions, to set the colour.*

three *To decorate wrapping paper, trace different types of writing on to tissue paper, using gold acrylic paint. Complement the wrapping paper with a bow of white or gold-trimmed organza (organdie) ribbon.*

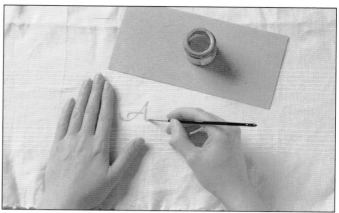

four *For the monogrammed hand towel, use paper cut-outs to plan your design. Tape the chosen letter flat on to a work surface. Lay the towel over the alphabet, and tape flat. Trace over the letter on to the towel with the fabric paint.*

five *If you wish to apply an initial to a chair or other piece of furniture, put carbon paper on to the back of the photocopied lettering or rub all over the back with a soft pencil. Then transfer this to the furniture by going over the outline with a harder pencil. Paint over the outline and leave to dry.*

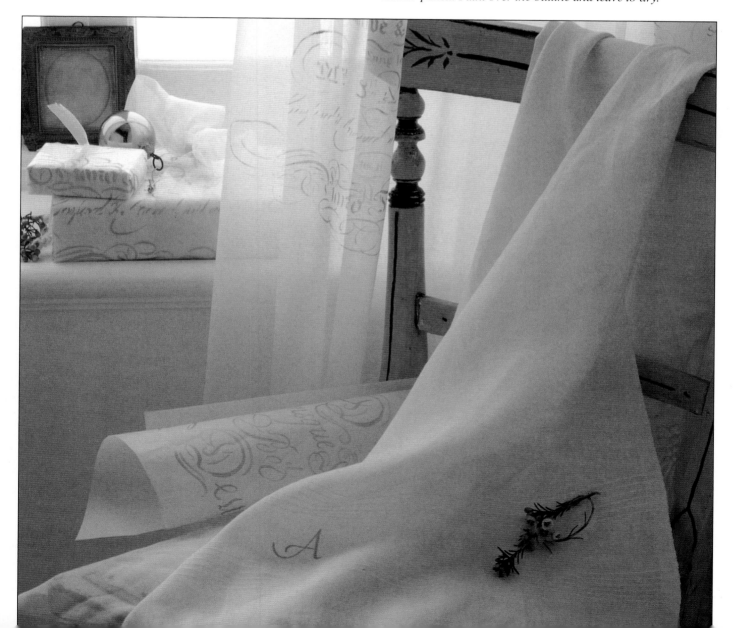

RIBBONS AND LACE

MAKE THE MOST OF A BEAUTIFUL PIECE of sari fabric or a superb lace panel by displaying it in a window so that the light shines through. A few hand-stitched lengths of ribbon will allow you to tie back the fabric to reveal as much or as little of the window and the view as you like. As the main fabric is very light and translucent, hang a length of white muslin (cheesecloth) behind it for extra privacy.

YOU WILL NEED

muslin (cheesecloth),
1½ x window width

iron-on hem fix
(such as Wundaweb)

iron

white tape

needle and matching sewing
thread

dowel, window width

2 cup hooks

scissors

cream linen ribbon

sari fabric or lace panel

one *Finish the hems on the muslin (cheesecloth) with iron-on hem fix, then sew lengths of white tape along the top to the dowel. Screw the hooks into the window frame and hang up the dowel rail. Tie the curtain on to the rail.*

two *Cut the ribbon into eight 25cm (10in) lengths and stitch four along the top edge of the sari fabric or lace panel. Stitch the others at intervals along the sides – their positions will depend on the size of the panel and the parts that you want to show off. You can also hide any defects when you tie them up in this way.* ➤

three *Tie the top ribbons to the rail using simple bows. Arrange them along the rail so that the fabric drapes over the window in the most appealing way.*

four *Tie up sections of the panel using the side ribbons. Experiment with different combinations, standing back from the window to check your adjustments until you are happy.*

EGYPTIAN DREAM

A PAIR OF COTTON SHEETS makes the most wonderful drape and all the seams are perfectly finished. The bigger the sheets, the more luxurious and elegant the window will look – drapes should always be generous. Wooden pegs can be wedged into a piece of old wooden floorboarding or driftwood – if you drill the holes at an angle, the fixing will be stronger as well as more decorative.

YOU WILL NEED

scissors

2.5m (2½yd) cotton tape

2 flat king-size cotton sheets

needle and white sewing thread

drill

length of floorboarding or driftwood, window width plus 15cm (6in) either side

6 old-fashioned wooden pegs

spirit (carpenter's) level

wallplugs and screws

screwdriver

one *With scissors, cut the cotton tape into six strips of equal length.*

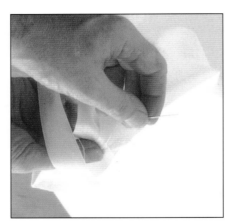

two *Divide the width of each sheet top by three and use the divisions as points to attach the tapes. Fold each tape in half and use small stitches to sew them to the top of the sheet.*

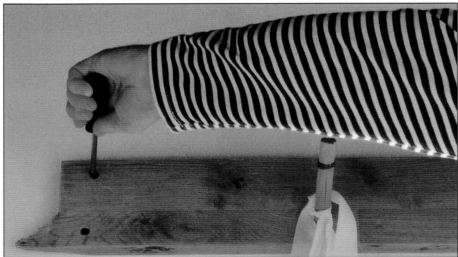

three *Drill six holes at equal distances along the floorboarding and wedge in the pegs. Drill a hole either end of the floorboarding and screw it into the wall, using a spirit (carpenter's) level to check it is straight, and appropriate fixings to secure it.*

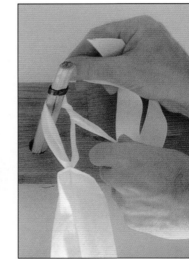

four *Tie the tapes securely and neatly to the pegs and arrange the drapes.*

WHITE MISCHIEF

SMALL DETAILS SUCH AS the curtain clips in this project make the important difference between an obvious and an elegant solution to curtain hanging. The fabric is a generously long piece, folded in half, allowing a drop 1½ times the length of the window – it really is a very simple, yet elegant example of window dressing! Small brass curtain clips fit over the rail and catch the fabric along the fold.

YOU WILL NEED

dowel, window width

woodstain

kitchen cloth

drill

wallplugs and nails

hammer

curtain clips

white muslin (cheesecloth)

wooden spear or a garden implement

one *Stain the length of dowel by shaking woodstain on to a soft cloth and rubbing the dowel with it until you achieve the effect you want.*

two *Drill two holes either side of the window in the wall and insert the wallplugs. Bang in the nails.*

three *Clip the fabric along the fold, leaving an equal distance between the clips. Thread the rings on to the dowel and place the dowel over the nails.*

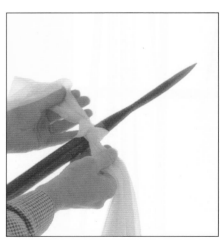

four *Spread the rings along the dowel so that the fabric falls in even drapes.*

five *Knot the front drop of fabric on to the end of the spear and prop this across the window.*

BILLOWING MUSLIN

FLOATY MUSLIN (CHEESECLOTH) IS one of the cheapest ways to cover a large window without blocking out all the light. The fabric here is in two pieces, each long enough to drape over the rail and down to the floor on both sides. One of the lengths was stamped with a sponge cut-out in the shape of a melon half. The two pieces were hung next to each other and knotted about halfway down so the stamped half crosses over to the other side.

YOU WILL NEED

tracing paper

pencil

thin cardboard, for template

block of high-density foam rubber (the type used for camping mattresses)

craft knife

2 lengths of muslin (cheesecloth)

2 bamboo poles, window width

sewing machine (optional)

needle

matching sewing thread

fabric paint: coffee-brown and dark brown

plate

paint roller or paintbrush

adhesive tape

drill, and masonry bit

wall plugs and cup hooks

bundle of natural-coloured raffia

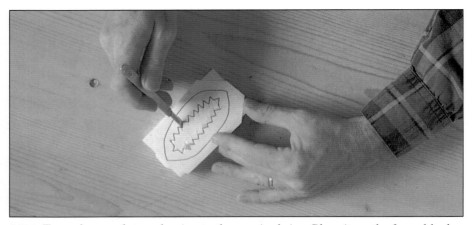

one *Trace the template, enlarging to the required size. Place it on the foam block, then cut around it. Scoop out the inner area, leaving the printing surface intact. Fold both of the muslin (cheesecloth) lengths in half. Form a channel along the top of each, about 5cm (2in) down from the fold. It must be the width of the two bamboo poles, as they will slide into it. Sew by machine or hand.*

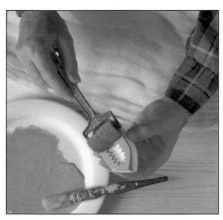

two *Put some of the coffee-brown fabric paint on to the plate and run the roller through it until it is thoroughly and evenly coated. Use the roller to ink the foam stamp.*

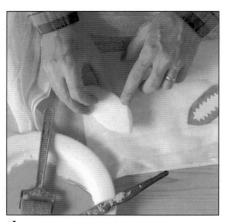

three *Start stamping the pattern, rotating the stamp in your hand each time you print. Leave more or less the same amount of space between prints.*

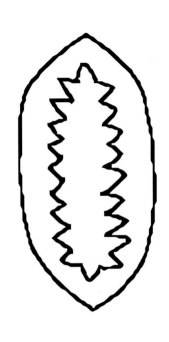

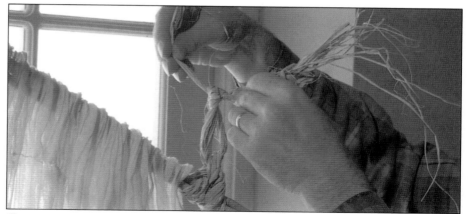

four *Stamp darker prints randomly among lighter ones. Fix the fabric paint according to the manufacturer's instructions. Tape over the ends of the bamboo poles so that they do not catch on the muslin, and slide them through the sewn channels in the curtains.*

five *Drill holes and insert the wall plugs and cup hooks in the top of the window recess, about 10–15cm (4–6in) in from the sides. Cut ten 45cm (18in) strips of raffia and use five on either side, twisted together into a rope, to bind the bamboo poles together in place of the tape. Use the loose ends to suspend the bamboo rail by tying them to the cup hooks. Tie a knot with the two curtains about halfway down their length. Experiment with different effects, but take your time over the positioning of the knot, its shape and the way the muslin drapes over it.*

INDIAN SUMMER

THIS WINDOW SEAT RECESS was given a touch of glamorous Eastern mystery by layering fine, silky sari lengths behind each other to build up to a gloriously rich colour. The sunlight picks up the gold embroidered flecks and braids, and the star lantern between the curtains casts its own magic spell. If you have never been in a sari shop, you will be amazed by the vast range of exquisitely patterned silks and voiles you can buy.

YOU WILL NEED

7 red and yellow sari lengths (or fewer)

braid, 7m (7yd) plus width of each sari for braid edging

iron-on hem fix (such as Wundaweb)

iron

needle

matching sewing thread

wooden curtain rail

drill

wall plugs and hooks

wrought-iron curtain rail

one *If the saris do not have braid edges, add them with iron-on hem fix. Cut the remaining braid into 14cm (5½in) lengths to make seven loops for each sari. Space them at equal distances along the tops, and slip stitch. Put the wooden curtain rail through all the loops of three saris and fix it into the recess with hooks. Hang the iron rail on the outer frame, and hang two saris on the left by threading their loops alternately so that one hangs in front. Hang the two other saris on the right.*

two *Separate the red and yellow saris, holding one in each hand about halfway down their length.*

three *Wrap the yellow one round the red one and knot them together. Arrange the folds of the knot so that the fabric tumbles away and spills to the floor.*

SHELL SHOCKED

AFTER HOLIDAYING, MAKE your shell collection into something really special. We have used them to decorate fine voile curtains, and added interest with eyelets along the top threaded with string loops. On this theme, an easy, effective way of trimming a wall is with a length of fine rope attached at dado-rail height. Fix a row of tiny shells above. To complete the look, paint a terracotta pot white and attach a small sand dollar to the front.

YOU WILL NEED

iron-on interfacing (optional)

tape measure

scissors

cotton voile, the required drop, and 4 x the window width

dressmaker's pins

needle and tacking thread

sewing machine

matching sewing thread

chrome eyelets

hammer

wooden block

rough natural string

glue gun and glue sticks

electric drill, with very fine drill bit (optional)

fine beading wire

beading needle (optional)

terracotta pot

matt white emulsion (latex) paint

household paintbrush

sand dollar shell

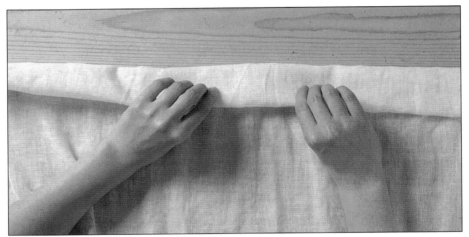

one *To give extra body to the headings of fine fabrics, cut a length of iron-on interfacing 5cm (2in) wide and bond it to the wrong side of the voile. Pin, tack, press and machine-stitch the heading across the top and the hem at the bottom. Then turn under a 1cm (½in) hem down each side. Pin, tack, press and sew. Mark the positions of the eyelets with pins.*

two *Fix the eyelets, following the manufacturer's instructions. Find a secure surface when hammering the eyelets in place.*

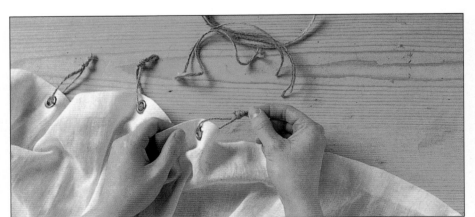

three *Cut equal lengths of string, thread the strings through the eyelets and knot the ends. Cut lengths of wire and use a glue gun to stick them on to the shells. Alternatively, drill holes in the shells. A combination of these methods may be helpful, depending on the shape of the shells. Position the shells on the curtains.*

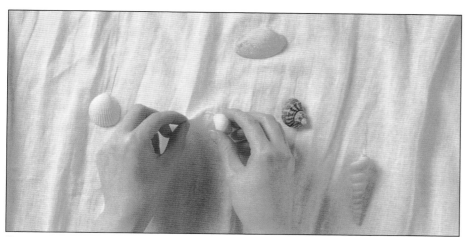

four *Use the beading wire to "sew" the shells on to the curtain by hand, as invisibly as possible.*

five *Paint the terracotta pot white. Put a little glue on the side of the pot and attach the sand dollar.*

BUTTONED BLANKETS

THESE BLANKETS WERE too brilliant to hide away under bedcovers so they were transformed into an attractive window treatment. They make good draught excluders and are simply rigged up on a couple of towel rails. You need a solid wall as the blankets are weighty. The blankets are doubled over and held with a row of large safety pins.

YOU WILL NEED

2 chrome towel rails

drill

wallplugs and extra-long screws

screwdriver

2 colourful wool blankets

10 large coloured buttons, to contrast with blanket colours

dressmaker's pins or double-sided tape

large safety pins

one *Fix the towel rails to the wall above the window, by drilling holes and inserting wallplugs. As towel rails are not long enough to cover the whole width, hang them at different heights.*

two *Fold both the blankets in half lengthways. Drape them over the curtain rails, to create a 30cm (12in) pelmet (valance) as shown. Take down the blankets. Decide upon the position of the buttons, trying them out by fixing them to the blankets with dressmaker's pins or with double-sided tape.*

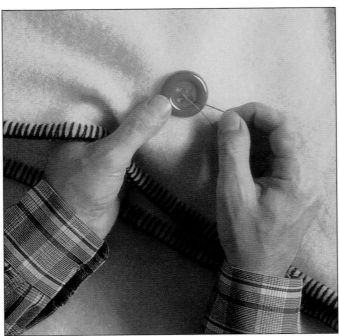

three *Stitch the buttons along the pelmet, just catching the first layer with a few stitches to secure the buttons, but without damaging the blanket.*

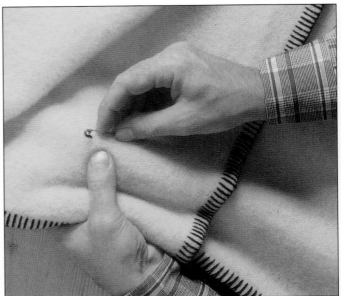

four *Pin a row of safety pins about halfway down the pelmet, on the underside where they won't show. Hang the blankets back in position. Re-pin carefully, so that each safety pin goes through the inside layer of the pelmet, and the outer layer of the curtain.*

ℬ IJOU BOUDOIR

BALLROOM DANCERS, bad-taste rockers, brides and prima ballerinas all love it – netting has that special star quality that windows sometimes need! You can cut, pleat, layer, scrunch and bunch it – there is nothing to sew and it is so light that many filmy, glamorous lengths can hang from a single strand of plastic-coated sprung wire.

Netting comes in all sorts of colours and the idea from this project could easily be translated into a completely stunning party window in dramatic purple or scarlet and black. Tie the the lengths of netting back with feather boas, strings of pearls or even kitsch diamanté dog collars to make the most glamorous window this side of Cannes.

YOU WILL NEED

pliers

4 eyelet hooks

2 lengths of plastic-coated sprung wire, window width

4m (4yd) each pink and white netting

scissors

fine wire

feather boa

fake pearl strands

one *Screw in an eyelet hook at the same height either side of the window recess.*

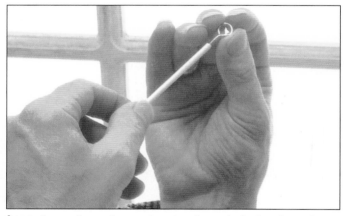

two *Loop the eyelet on the wire through the hooks and stretch the wire taut across the window.*

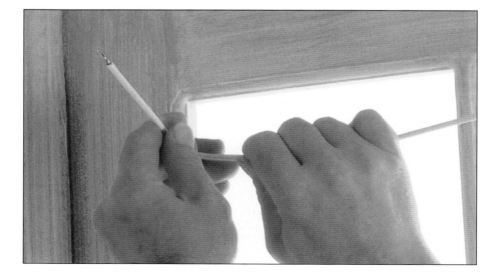

three *Repeat the process, positioning the second wire about 8cm (3in) in front of the first (of course, this distance will be dictated by the depth of your window recess).*

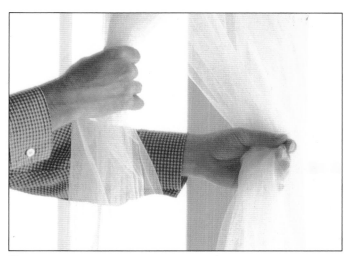

four *Cut the netting in half. Feed half the length of the pink netting over the back wire. Set aside the rest of the pink netting.*

five *Feed the length of the white netting over the back wire, next to the pink netting. Pull both lengths of netting into shape, making a double layer with each.*

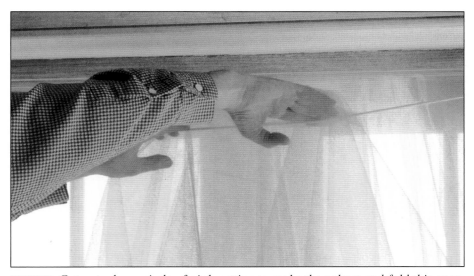

six *Hang the other layer of pink netting over the front wire.*

seven *Cut out a large circle of pink netting to make the pelmet and fold this over the front wire to create a semi-circle.*

eight *Cut long strips of netting and scrunch them into rosettes. Tuck them between the wires. You will find that the netting is very easy to scrunch into good shapes. Pleat up the semi-circular pelmet, adding folds and creases along the wire as you go.*

CONTINUED OVER ➤

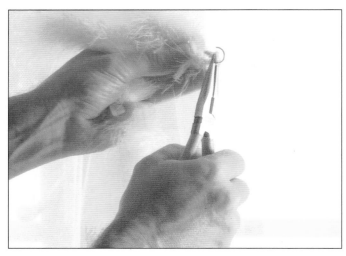

nine *Make big white rosettes to go into the corners by scrunching up the white netting. Tuck them into the wire to secure and smooth them out to make a pleasing shape.*

ten *Twist the fine wire into connecting rings and use them to attach the feather boa along the curve of the netting pelmet.*

eleven *Drape the strands of fake pearls from the centre of the front wire and tie up the ends.*

Right: One of the great advantages of netting is that it is easy to handle, and is quite forgiving. If you don't like the first shape you have made, smooth it out and scrunch it up again. These rosettes are simply tucked between the front and back.

ARTIST'S STUDIO

THIS IS THE IDEAL WAY to cover a large studio window, and as canvas comes in so many sizes, you're bound to find a piece to fit your window. If you have never previously considered the possibility of becoming a painter, then this is a good way to start – curtains can also be art!

Here, chalks were used to draw on to the canvas and change the flat panel into a boldly gathered backdrop. You could use this idea as your inspiration, or you could flick colours on it in Jackson Pollock style, or simply add a few minimalist squiggles. If your window receives a lot of light, you may want to suspend a builder's dust-sheet in front of the window. This will provide a lining for the main curtain.

YOU WILL NEED

canvas, 1½ x window width

chalks or acrylic paints and paintbrush

drill

4 chunky garage hooks

screwdriver

metal cleat

rope

double-sided carpet tape

brass eyelets

hammer

one *Draw, paint or print on to the canvas using whatever style or design you have chosen – the bolder the better, as the canvas will cover a large surface area.*

two *Fix the garage hooks securely into the wall above the window, spaced at equal intervals.*

three *Screw the cleat to the wall, about halfway down the side of the window, then wind one end of the rope around it several times.*

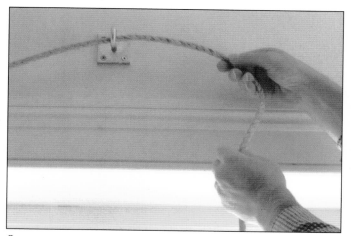

four *Take the long end of the rope up and through the hooks along the top.*

five *Pull the rope taut and tie it on to the end hook. Then fix the seams and eyelets on to the canvas following the manufacturer's instructions.*

six *Thread the rope through the first eyelet from behind, allowing about 16cm (6¼in) between the hook and the eyelet. Then, leaving the same distance again, twist a loop in the rope and put it on the hook.*

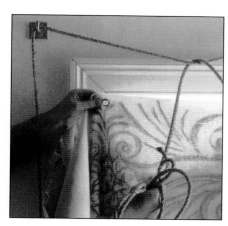

seven *Take the rope down and through the back of the next eyelet, then up and over the back taut rope, which now forms a 'rail' for the rope to rest on.*

eight *When you reach the end of the curtain, take the rope through the last hook.*

nine *Take the rope straight down the side of the window and tie it neatly on to the cleat.*

CONTINUED OVER ➤

ten *Cut an extra length of rope and hook it over one of the top centre hooks so that one length falls to the front and the other to the back of the canvas. Gather the canvas up and get hold of both ends of the rope. Tie these together in a knot and leave the ends dangling free.*

Above: The knot holding the curtain back from the window allows the light to come through.

Above: Allow plenty of canvas so that it spills generously out on to the floor below the window.

Above: The knotted rope forms an additional decorative element in its own right.

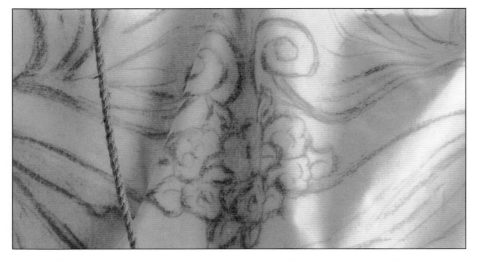

Above: The natural colour of the canvas enhances the subtle colours of the design.

JAPANESE SCREEN

THIS SCREEN IS THE perfect treatment for a minimalist room scheme. It lets you hide from the outside world, yet you can still benefit from the light filtering through. The screen is made from a simple wooden garden trellis, painted matt black, with heavyweight tracing paper stapled behind it. You can cut the trellis to fit your window recess, but always do it to the nearest square so it looks balanced. The paper is stapled behind the struts.

YOU WILL NEED

garden trellis
blackboard paint
household paintbrush
heavyweight tracing paper
staple gun
craft knife
red emulsion (latex) paint
drill, with wood bit
2 eyelets
tape measure
wire coat hanger
wire cutters
pliers
2 picture hooks

one *Paint the trellis black and leave to dry. Blackboard paint creates a perfectly matt finish, but other matt or gloss paints can be used. Staple sheets of tracing paper on to the back of the trellis. If necessary, trim the tracing paper with a craft knife so that no overlaps or joins are visible from the front. It must look like a single sheet.*

two *For added interest, paint one square red and leave to dry. Drill a very fine hole in the top of the trellis, at the first strut in from each end.*

three *Screw an eyelet into each hole. Measure the length of the window to determine how long the hooks for hanging should be. The base of the screen should touch the window frame below. Cut two pieces of coat-hanger wire to the correct length for the hooks, then hang the screen on these from picture rail hooks.*

BUTTERFLY MONTAGE

SURREALISM AND THE WORK of artists such as Ernst, Escher, and Magritte inspire surprising ways of depicting familiar objects in designs for montages. This butterfly floor could easily have been made using motifs of flowers, boats or chairs. Strong lines are important, and there are books of wonderful line drawings available. Lay the motifs down in an ordered pattern. Here the design suggests the flight of butterflies. Protect the montage from wear and tear, by applying half a dozen coats of varnish.

YOU WILL NEED

light-coloured emulsion (latex) paint

household paintbrushes

paper motifs

craft knife

self-healing cutting mat

wallpaper paste

indelible felt-tipped pen or fine artist's brush and oil-based paints

matt varnish

one *Make sure your floor is completely smooth. If necessary, lay a hardboard or marine-plywood floor. Paint the floor a light colour so that the motifs will show up. Photocopy your chosen image(s) in at least seven sizes, ranging from quite small to fairly large.*

two *Using a craft knife and a cutting mat, carefully cut out every image.*

three *Decide on the positions of your images and glue them in place with wallpaper paste.*

four *Add remaining fine details with a fine artist's brush and/or an indelible felt-tipped pen. Finish by applying at least six coats of varnish to be sure of its durability (some acrylic varnishes dry very quickly) or apply a very strong floor varnish.*

GILDED CHAIR

MANY A BEAUTIFUL BENTWOOD chair is relegated to the attic because its cane seat is damaged. Re-caning is expensive and it is hard to find skilled craftsmen; it often seems easier and cheaper to buy a new chair. This is a shame because a bentwood chair can become the star of a room, with some effort but little expense, by setting in a solid seat. Once the cane has been removed, the chair looks wonderful with gold-leaf decoration.

YOU WILL NEED

wooden chair

craft knife

small screwdriver or bradawl

4 wooden blocks

pencil

saw

drill, with wood bit

8 wood screws

screwdriver

sheet of paper

scissors

sheet of plywood

masking tape

jigsaw (optional)

medium-grade sandpaper

gold size

household paintbrushes

gold leaf or 2 x 25-sheet
packets of gold Dutch metal

clean, soft paintbrush

clean, dry cloth

varnish

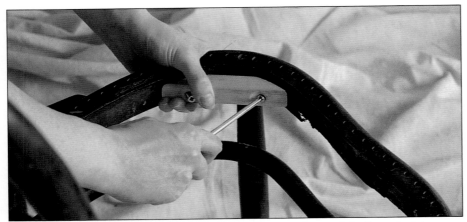

one *If the seat needs repairing, cut away the cane with a craft knife and pick out the remaining strands with a screwdriver or bradawl. To make the supporting corner blocks, hold the pieces of wood inside each corner, mark the shape on the wood and then cut the pieces to shape. Hold a corner block in position and drill through it into the chair. Screw the block into position. Repeat for all four corners.*

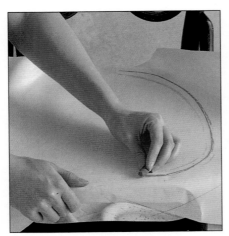

two *Lay the paper over the seat and trace the shape. Cut out to create the template. Tape the template to the plywood and draw around it.*

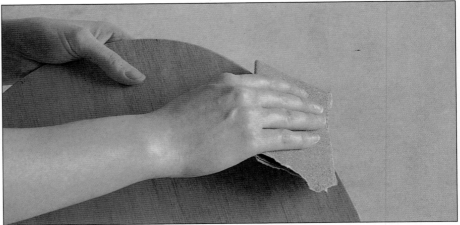

three *Cut around the pencil line. (A timber merchant can do this for you if you do not have a jigsaw.) Sand the edges of the wooden seat to fit and drop it into place. Prepare the chair for gilding by sanding all the surfaces lightly. Roughening the wood helps the size to adhere.*

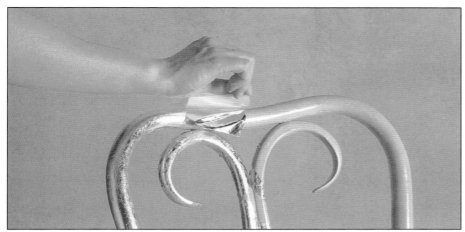

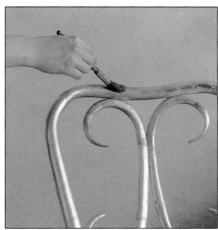

four *Paint the chair with size and allow it to dry. Follow the manufacturer's recommendations. Holding the gold leaf by the backing paper, lay a sheet on the chair. With a clean, dry brush, rub the gold leaf on to the chair. Continue until the chair is covered. It is very important that both the brush and your hands are clean and dry.*

five *Rub the chair with a clean, dry cloth to remove any loose flakes. Finally, to protect the gold leaf, seal the whole chair with varnish.*

GUSTAVIAN CHAIR

PRETTY GUSTAVIAN PAINTED CHAIRS give a lightness and elegance to bedroom furniture. They are expensive because few are available outside Scandinavia, where they originated. Create your own by painting a wooden chair of classic shape. It should have a padded seat, pretty outlines and enough space on the back rest for a motif. Traditional colours are greys, dark blues, aquamarine, honey-yellow and red, as well as white.

YOU WILL NEED

classic wooden chair

medium- and fine-grade sandpaper

emulsion (latex) paint: white, blue and black

household paintbrush

fine and medium paintbrushes

monogram motif

tracing paper

soft and hard pencils

masking tape

clear matt varnish

typeface or script samples (e.g. from a calligraphy book)

large sheet of paper

scissors

1m (1yd) of 137cm (54in) (or twice seat-cover width) white cotton fabric

indelible laundry or fabric marker

staple gun

needle

matching sewing thread

gold and silver spray paint

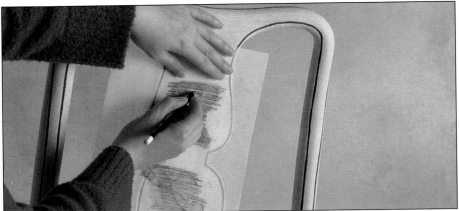

one *Lightly sand the chair with medium-grade sandpaper to make a key for the paintwork. Paint the chair with an undercoat of white emulsion (latex). Mix blue-grey emulsion then, using the fine paintbrush, carefully outline the shape of the back of the chair. Add similar detailing to the seat and legs. Leave to dry. Trace your chosen letters and scrolls. Turn the tracing paper over, and rub all over the back with the soft pencil. Turn it over, position it on the chair back and tape it in place. Go over the outlines with a hard pencil to transfer them to the chair.*

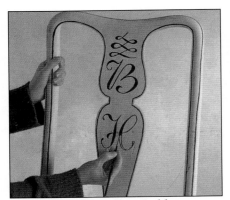

two *Fill in the outlines in blue-grey with the medium paintbrush. Refer to your original reference for where the brush strokes should be thicker.*

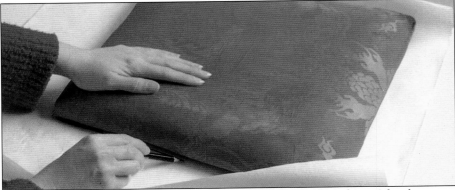

three *Allow to dry. Apply a coat of matt varnish (water-based varnishes have very short drying times). Cut a piece of paper roughly the size of the chair seat pad, to give you an idea of the area to which you need to apply lettering. Photocopy type alphabets or sections of script, enlarging them, if necessary.*

four *Cut up the script and arrange the pieces on the paper. Put the paper against a brightly lit window, and smooth the fabric over the design. Fix to the glass with masking tape. Using the fabric marker, carefully trace over the letters. Cover the seat pad with the fabric, securing it on the back with staples. Take a second piece of fabric, just smaller than the underside of the seat, turn under the edges and sew in place to cover the staples.*

five *Lightly spray over the whole seat with gold paint. Repeat with silver. Replace the seat pad in the chair. Lightly sand the paint with fine-grade sandpaper to give it a charming, slightly aged effect.*

FABRIC-SWATHED CHAIR

THIS EFFECT IS STYLISH and practical and yet needs no sewing skills. None of the usual difficulties caused by the need for washing of fitted covers apply, so you can capitalize on the sheer drama that is created by brilliant white. A generous quantity of fabric is the only essential; this project uses a king-size, pure cotton sheet, which is ready-hemmed, but you can use any wide, preferably washable, fabric that is soft enough to knot and tie. Why not consider this as a stunning addition to your Christmas scheme, by wrapping the dining chairs in red silk?

YOU WILL NEED

chair

fabric, such as cotton sheet

sewing machine
(optional)

one *You need at least twice, and preferably three times, as much fabric as the width of your chair. Hem the fabric, if necessary. Throw the fabric over the chair and centre it.*

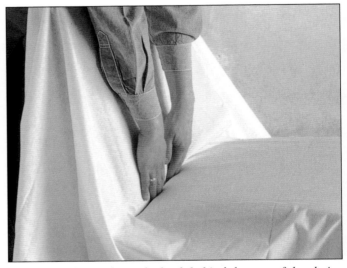

two *Tuck fabric down the back behind the seat of the chair. If the chair has arms, do this all around the seat, so that the cover doesn't pull when you sit on the chair.*

three *Sweep the fabric round to the back of the chair, allowing it to drape.*

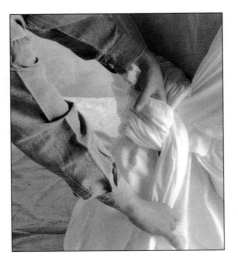

four *Tie a knot, making sure that the fabric is an even length on both sides and that you have attractive folds and drapes at the sides. Try to tie the knot confidently in one go: otherwise the fabric can look tortured and may be crumpled. Remember that the fabric should cascade down from the knot.*

STOOL WITH WOOD

THIS IS A VERY SIMPLE and yet effective look, which does not involve any complicated techniques. The wood mouldings used here are available in a considerable range from your local timber merchant or hardware store and are intended for embellishing doors and panelling. However, they also give instant texture to otherwise plain objects, lending them unexpected style.

YOU WILL NEED

wooden stool

white undercoat paint, if necessary

household paintbrushes

ruler

pencil

wooden mouldings

glue gun

oil-based brown paint, mixed with 2 parts matt glaze (scumble)

creamy white oil paint

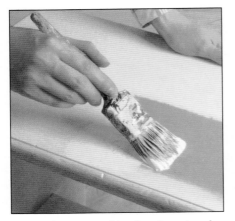

one *If your stool is already painted in strong colours, paint it white to give a neutral base colour.*

two *Draw a central grid in pencil on the sides of the stool and decide on the positioning of the mouldings. Glue them on to the surface. Either curves or angles are suitable.*

three *Using the brown glaze and working continuously in one direction (to simulate the grain of the wood), paint the whole stool. Allow to dry.*

four *Using a pale wash of cream, paint over the mouldings. Remove some of the glaze while still wet with a dry brush, to give a limed appearance.*

INDEX

ACKNOWLEDGEMENTS
The publishers would like to
thank the following for
creating additional projects in
this book:

Andrea Spencer: pages 44–5,
48–9, 60–1, 72–3; and
Catherine Tully: pages 86–7,
90–1, 92–3.

Additional photography by:
Michelle Garrett: pages 12 b,
13 t; Gloria Nicol: page 9 b;
Lizzie Orme: page 11 t; and
Spike Powell: pages 8 t b, 9 t.